CON

*In loving memory
of Mum, Dad and Christine
and
for Donna, Charlotte and Tiffany,
now.*

INVITATION

One day
it *will* happen –
that Italian feast in the garden:

long tables
under pergolas
clustered with grapes;

pasta, vino, dancing
and music – oh yes – *definitely* music;
Gigli, Pavarotti *and* Sinatra, capisce?

But most importantly, on the guest list, you.

And when the stragglers
are laughing down the lane
to their taxis and cars,

we'll sit
by the little gnarled apple tree,
as thudding moths shake the lanterns,

and I'll thank you, then,
with the backing of the open heavens
until the dying of the last star.

HERON

You wouldn't be surprised if you heard
the clanking of metal when he took off.

Perhaps you've wandered into Jurassic Park?
Ridiculous, this gangling oddball.

But not that skewer of a beak
you imagine a fish seeing

through the shattering glass,
the whirl of water.

HARE

Alone
in a fallow field
as though he can't be seen.
(And you amazed, again,
at just how big they are.)

Not the brightest of course:
like jay-walking pheasants
or partridges, losing it,
just when the gun's being cocked.

But you *really* like him. Just know
he'd be a riot if he could talk –
how well you'd get on.
And those semaphore ears!

Now he's off again:
going like the clappers
over the furrows, doing that
buckled
bicycle wheel number

as though
just for the hell of it. As though,
even through
those clenched gnashers,

he just can't keep it all in.

SPLASH

by David Hockney

By this time
the diver's
left the pool *and* the picture

those glass doors are sliding shut
wet footprints
drying in the sun

and I'm wondering
just what it is
that I love about this painting.

It's hot and blue, and, well,
Californian, I suppose.
The burnt hills roll away.

And I'm trying to figure
how anything grows here at all.
I look again at the pool

and the sky, wonder if the water
really does have those dancing circles of light –
yep, they're there all right.

And that palm. All in that blaze
of brilliant blue stillness
that he nicked, surely,

from Matisse?

A YORKSHIRE PARABLE

I went to see the wisest man in the world –
he lived above a shop in Cleckheaton.
A nice man, he offered me tea and biscuits
before we got down to business.

Is there an omniscient being? I asked him,
one who shares an intimate
relationship with each and every one of us?
I wouldn't really know, he said.

Well, do you believe in an afterlife?
A heaven, perhaps: or maybe reincarnation?
It would be nice, he mused –
pushing over the chocolate éclairs.

Realising I was getting nowhere with this,
I wandered over to the window
and watched as cold November light
set fire to the trees across the road.

Nice day, I ventured.
Now you're getting somewhere, he replied.

FLIGHT

It was one of those days:

moaning people,
        tragedy on tv,
                moaning me.

Then a 747 splitting the blue.

So I jumped up,
        ran along the vapour trail,
                hammered at the windows to let me in.

ON THE CLEVELAND WAY

You've come this far
and surely that's a good thing.
A few scrapes sure
but sat on this rock
the view's good
and what with the sandwiches and coffee
and the warmth percolating
through layers of gortex and cotton
you're up for it all right
though glad of this short rest.

Looking back
you blink into the sun –
impressed at the distance covered –
but that cliff-edge walk
round the headland
is sickening from this perspective.
Standing up with the odd creak
it's the path ahead that draws you on
towards the signal station,
the copse in the distance.

ENCOUNTER

for all at Scarborough Library

Nipping through the snicket
to the library – between the bank
and McDonald's – it could have been
a scene from *The Third Man*:
a bloke in a trench coat
and fedora, static for a spell
on his disability scooter,
was lighting up a ciggie
in his cupped hands.
He raised his eyebrows
as I passed (in a sort of recognition
or solidarity), and I thought immediately
of Orson Wells and that music.
But then felt a great affection and pride:
him, tackling his situation so stoically
and, relishing the irony,
hoped he would really enjoy his cigarette.
Then the passage ended. And blinded
temporarily by the sun, I turned sharp left
past the computer suite, up the steps,
and in through the new automatic doors.

ON NOT BEING TED HUGHES

As though bent on demonstrating stupidity,
against the advice of my wife,
against the increasingly *vocal* advice of my wife,

in the summer-glutted garden,
by the red-hot pokers and the Cordyline
I picked it up: a bank vole.

It looked so dozy in the sun,
seemingly stunned, like a dormouse.

But against all categories of sense,
in complete ignorance of its being
and the *screaming* of my wife,
I picked it up.

He would have known. Ted. Oh aye,
he would have known all right –
he wouldn't have picked it up.

Years later I'm the family joke,
always something for them to smile at:

'silly bugger…picking it up…'

AMY WINEHOUSE IS A TIME TRAVELLER

That voice. That look. That talent.
Think Bessie Smith, Mahaliah Jackson or Aretha;
not Madonna or those X-Factor clones.

Beamed down from Bourbon St.,
twenties Chicago,
or the business end of a cotton field.

But don't go while you're visiting us Amy.
Don't do a Hank Williams or an Elvis,
or come a cropper like Jimi and Janis.

Be our Billy Holliday
but *live* Amy.
Live.

WHERE EAGLES DARE

I've nobbled Richard Burton
because I want his voice. I want
to say – have *always* wanted to say:

Broadsword calling Danny Boy.
Broadsword calling Danny Boy.

I want to curl my lip like his.
I want to squint slightly, flare
my nostrils then growl:

Broadsword calling Danny Boy.
Broadsword calling Danny Boy.

And Clint. Clint Eastwood.
I want to order fresh-faced Clint
around and say repeatedly:

Broadsword calling Danny Boy.
Broadsword calling Danny Boy.

In fact, after a while,
because of my dearth of lines
I'm rumbled. But I don't mind.

I've become Richard Burton,
doing a Richard Burton,
in a Richard Burton movie.

UNDERTAKER

for Martyn Threapleton

You almost wanted to sign up early –
 put yourself in his hands.

With his gnarled benevolence
and graveyard humour

you knew the job would be sorted
as soon as you made that first call.

Okay. A tidy ceremony may not be
the answer to everyone's prayers.

But when the pressure was on,
he seemed like some rugged saint,

who was not only more capable,
but knew exactly what to do –

just when you needed it most.

DOMICILIUM

There's 'ell on 'cos Tiff's lost her dinosaurs,
the neighbour's murdering Pavarotti,
and the washing machine's locked on spin.

We're all sat around like outpatients,
there's a fleece drip-drying over the sink,
and the bathroom's a rainforest again.

The un-killable telly's blinking in the corner
and we desperately need a plan –
but no-one can be arsed.

You think about doing a runner
or making a break for it to the shed
but even that seems too far to go.

DOPPELGÄNGERS

for Martin Arnold

Amazing who you see on the street:
today, Van Morrison in Asda;
last month, Kylie
selling ciggies in Tesco's.

I've been pursued down The Headrow
to Briggate by Karl Marx.
And in a café last summer,
Madonna serving sausage and chips.

It can be disconcerting though –

Bono up a ladder. Bill Gates in Oxfam.
Richard Burton in a Reliant Robin.

NOT QUITE BIRDSONG

A butcher where I worked once
was a whistler – you know the type:
aggressive, soulless. I'd stand around
being useless somewhere planning his death.

Days at his block and bacon slicer
rending the air, making his shrill statement.
Clocking on to clocking off –
Colonel Bogey or *The Sheik of Araby.*

And you could tell he worked at it –
thought he was good. I'd think
of his family, how they coped.
Thought about sympathy cards.

And the other butchers? Surely
he was pushing his luck
next to all those knives and meat-hooks.
Not to mention the mincer.

A SNAPSHOT FROM 1917

Midday, probably. A tea-break
certainly: granddad Murphy
holding court among laughing soldiers,
a raised mug and thumbs up to the camera.

And taken beforehand, but where?
Away from the trenches it implies
but doesn't reveal, it could be a snapshot
of a works' outing. Uproarious:

sleeves rolled, cigs in mouths, laughing
like loons; like a day out at Blackpool
or larking about on Brighton pier. And noise –
what would it be? Birds? Maybe music?

No doubt they'd sing or whistle to themselves.
And there would surely be the tenor
who'd impress them all upon request,
which would be often.

FLAMINGO LAND

Cracking some gag about tomato juice
outside 'Drac's Diner', I'm Harry Houdini
escaping from the family rucksack. Shouting
"I'll catch you up by the Zebras!" I collapse

on a bench. A woman's yelling "Ro-ry!"
as grown-ups go skipping by with their kids
till superego's wagging finger
puts them sharply back in step.

A wrist-slashing jingle repeats itself so that
I see the attendant losing it,
ramming the throttle on full pelt and running
screaming into the Lion pit.

Those cockatoos seem happy enough,
and a red-arsed monkey's
attempting to brain another with a stick
while a third looks on masturbating.

All things considered, it's quite heroic really,
families making the best of it under
an August thunderscape – though Rory's
mother's at it again (what could he be up to?).

Then at 'Thunder Mountain', I pass a man dressed
as a pterodactyl, and a strapping young lass
in t-shirt and shorts with an ad across her chest
which I try not to read.

MALLORY

for Eric Sinclair

They found him
still clinging on after sixty years.
Dead, of course, but what bottle:
shinning up there
as though it were Scafell
on a good day.

And no *Berghaus* then. More like:
pass my corduroy jacket
I'm off up Annapurna,
best take some water, though,
I'll drink it at the top.

For God's sake!
We get wrapped up in gortex and fleeces,
jump in the *Fourtrack* (with rhinos on the side),
just to get half a dozen eggs and the paper!

Praise be to courage, to the adventurous spirit.

I look out at the sodden garden,
chart my journey to the shed.

OVER THE WIRE

Tense, to say the least, I tracked down
and found the ward he was on –

saw him lying on an end-bed
reading a fishing magazine.

Then halfway towards him his shout:
Under that bed, man – Billy thinks he's a crocodile!

After being scraped from the ceiling
then acting sensibly on his discharge,

we laughed insanely
all the way down the gravel drive,

constantly looking over our shoulders
for a possee of running white coats.

ALBERT

The Norbreck Hotel, Scarborough, 1968.

Poached from a paper round
to be a porter's assistant –
your assistant, weekends and holidays –
I worked there because *you* worked there.

Everybody loved you: small, skinny,
National Health specs; probably mid-fifties,
but to me, at fourteen, you were Methuselah.
And so funny! You'd slap a trailing leg to bring it in line,
or chase a pea around your plate, moaning
how hard life was – that even vegetables
gave you the runaround.

A Bradford man, you were football mad,
which explains why, four years later,
you turned up at Valley Parade to watch me play.
We met after the game: *You did all right lad*.
But then you would say that.
Then we lost touch. As you do.

Until today that is, when, walking down
memory lane past the hotel, I see you staring
owl-like through a window,
waiting for the coaches to arrive.

SUMMER

A garden breathing and just looking
at you. Heat turning bricks red,
keeping butterflies fluttering
and torturing dogs.

The shed squats in a corner
hoarding its tools;
and the gazebo down the far end
whispers long cool drinks and bourgeoisie.

But soon the days will shorten
back towards the lock of winter.

Till then, red-hot pokers burn,
grass demands the mower twice a week,
the vigorous hawthorn shields us from the lane

and a cat, in its own time and measure,
moves across the lawn.

WINTER

When pulling on jeans is an act of heroism,
when the garden's a no-man's land
and they're topping themselves in Scandinavia,

it's winter.

When the lane becomes The Cresta Run,
when trees are brass rubbings and the copse
a cold kingdom you visit with the dog,

it's winter.

When it's anti-freeze, pipe-lagging and balaclavas
(if you dare), when you can tot up the stars, stay in bed longer,
and when even the earth's curled up into a ball,

it's winter.

CROSSING

Walking past
the other day
with the family
brought it all back;
forty-eight years wiped
and there I was,
sandals and shorts,
and cradled in my arms –
that cream and brown
cabin cruiser.

The tiny pond
I remembered
as a sea. And the *thrill*:
setting her off, whirring,
from one of those little rocky inlets.
But then always
the agony of waiting,
as she'd search back
towards me from you, dad,
on the other side.

THEATRE OF DREAMS

I - SIR MATT

Old Trafford, Manchester, 1970

A voice like gravel soaked in honey:
Hello, there son.
So this is what God's like.

Outside the office window,
the grey wash of Stretford skyline
was suddenly Technicolor;

like that scene from *Mary Poppins*
where Dick Van Dyke
dances with the penguins

and it's as if you've had
a tab of acid
dropped in your tea.

2 - DENIS

The Cliff, Manchester, 1970

Keep it to yourself, son!
His laughing response
to my surname.

As wick as he was on the pitch,
everything around him
seemed slow, dull.

And those lifts into Manchester
when he'd catch a green light,
I half expected his salute through the sunroof!

He drove a cherry red Jag
like Inspector Morse's – only untidier:
kid's toys and health foods in the back.

He could have done stand-up:
wise-cracking with passing fans
when the lights were on red

the only thing it seemed to me
that had *any* chance of stopping him.

3 - NOBBY

The Cliff, Manchester, 1970

Nipping smartly past you
I was soon flat on my arse:
Can't get away with that 'ere son!

Then after you'd been struck on the head
by a Charlton thunderbolt – a worried Bobby
helping you up – your brilliant simile:

like a fucking bread pudding that bastard!

And later still, when playing out your career
with Middlesborough Reserves, I zipped past you again
one freezing, flood-lit night and scored: honours even.

Not that it mattered.
I mean, three years earlier,
you'd left your mark on me forever.

4 - BEST

The Cliff, Manchester, 1970

Too overawed to speak
so I brushed shoulders
as we trooped off from training.

You signed autographs
for young girls who'd slipped through the gates,
as I bent down and fiddled with a lace.

Then, amazingly, we were alone.
You in front – my fourth person of The Trinity:
that gunslinger waddle; head slightly to one side;

as though carrying some brilliantly jewelled cross,
the price you had to pay
for re-defining how a game could be played.

Me? Third division only, I'm afraid
(and not long there either),
with a cross of my own to bear

and a grave lesson to learn – namely this:
that I could never, ever, be me
as long as I was trying to be you.

MADRID

It happens to everyone sooner or later:
that time alone when, by chance or design,
we measure the span of the heavens.

Here for instance on this balcony in Spain:
a glut of mod-cons in the bedroom behind,
I look out over a sleeping pool
towards a line of hills kept visible
by the sleepless city.

But the stars are different here.

Back in Yorkshire they're blunt and dependable.
Only reckoned with when the dog's let out to pee,
long after the kids've been put to bed
with us knackered, half plugged into
a jabbering telly, not really talking so much
as together.